BIOGRAPHIES *of the* AMERICAN REVOLUTION

BENJAMIN FRANKLIN, JOHN ADAMS, JOHN PAUL JONES, AND MORE

BIOGRAPHIES *of the* AMERICAN REVOLUTION

BENJAMIN FRANKLIN, JOHN ADAMS, JOHN PAUL JONES, AND MORE

Edited by Michael Anderson

Britannica®
Educational Publishing

IN ASSOCIATION WITH

ROSEN
EDUCATIONAL SERVICES

Published in 2013 by Britannica Educational Publishing
(a trademark of Encyclopædia Britannica, Inc.)
in association with Rosen Educational Services, LLC
29 East 21st Street, New York, NY 10010.

Distributed exclusively by Rosen Educational Services.
For a listing of additional Britannica Educational Publishing titles, call toll free (800) 237-9932.

First Edition

Britannica Educational Publishing
J.E. Luebering: Director, Core Reference Group, Encyclopædia Britannica
Adam Augustyn: Assistant Manager, Encyclopædia Britannica

Anthony L. Green: Editor, Compton's by Britannica
Michael Anderson: Senior Editor, Compton's by Britannica
Andrea R. Field: Senior Editor, Compton's by Britannica
Sherman Hollar: Associate Editor, Compton's by Britannica

Marilyn L. Barton: Senior Coordinator, Production Control
Steven Bosco: Director, Editorial Technologies
Lisa S. Braucher: Senior Producer and Data Editor
Yvette Charboneau: Senior Copy Editor
Kathy Nakamura: Manager, Media Acquisition

Rosen Educational Services
Shalini Saxena: Editor
Nelson Sá: Art Director
Cindy Reiman: Photography Manager
Karen Huang: Photo Researcher
Brian Garvey: Designer, Cover Design
Introduction by Shalini Saxena

Library of Congress Cataloging-in-Publication Data

Biographies of the American Revolution: Benjamin Franklin, John Adams, John Paul Jones,
and more/edited by Michael Anderson.—1st ed.
    p. cm.—(Impact on America—collective biographies)
"In association with Britannica Educational Publishing, Rosen Educational Services."
Includes bibliographical references and index.
ISBN 978-1-61530-685-5 (library binding)
1. United States—History—Revolution, 1775–1783—Biography—Juvenile literature.
2. United States—Biography—Juvenile literature. I. Anderson, Michael, 1972–
E206.B56 2011
973.3092'2—dc23
[B]

2011046358

Manufactured in the United States of America

Cover, p. 3 Comstock/Thinkstock; cover, p. 3 (inset) © www.istockphoto.com/Joe Cicak (Benjamin
Franklin), Stock Montage/Archive Photos/Getty Images (John Paul Jones); back cover © www.istock-
photo.com/Sodafish bvba; interior background © www.istockphoto.com/oliopi (geometric), © www.
istockphoto.com/Bill Noll (floral)

CONTENTS

31

41

70

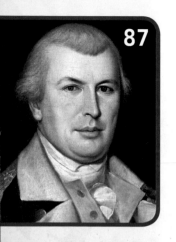

87

110

130

INTRODUCTION

The path to freedom—freedom from tyranny, oppression, or injustice—is rarely straightforward and is often riddled with obstacles. Individuals around the world and throughout the centuries have fought bravely for liberty and for what they believe to be justly theirs, many never living to see the fruits of their labors. The story of the independent American nation begins with a number of such men and women—including future presidents, international freedom fighters, and ordinary Americans from all walks of life—whose lives and contributions to the American Revolution are chronicled in this volume.

The seeds of the American Revolution had been planted around the time of the French and Indian War, several years before the Revolution broke out in 1775. The British, who then governed the colonies that would one day become the United States, had unjustly begun to tax the colonists and interfere with their trade and industry in order to help pay for the earlier war. Colonists increasingly began refusing to comply with such unfair tax practices as the Stamp Act and pushed more and more for full independence from Britain.

FREEDOM IS A LIGHT
FOR WHICH MANY MEN HAVE DIED IN DARKNESS

IN UNMARKED GRAVES WITHIN
THIS SQUARE LIE THOUSANDS
OF UNKNOWN SOLDIERS OF
WASHINGTON'S ARMY WHO DIED
OF WOUNDS AND SICKNESS DURING
THE REVOLUTIONARY WAR

THE INDEPENDENCE AND LIBERTY
YOU POSSESS ARE THE WORK OF
JOINT COUNCILS AND JOINT
EFFORTS OF COMMON DANGERS,
SUFFERINGS AND SUCCESS.
WASHINGTON'S FAREWELL ADDRESS SEPT. 17, 1796

The Tomb of the Unknown Soldier in Washington Square in Philadelphia, Pa., honors George Washington and the many unknown soldiers who gave their lives during the American Revolution and helped make possible the colonial victory against the British. **mary981/ Shutterstock.com**

Some of the most prominent voices of the Revolution belong to widely recognized names, including Benjamin Franklin, John Adams, Thomas Jefferson, and George Washington—better known, perhaps, as some of the nation's Founding Fathers. All were active in the Continental Congress, which made important decisions regarding the colonies' dealings with Britain and the direction of the country they hoped to form. Most of them also signed the Declaration of Independence and participated in the creation of the U.S. Constitution. From Franklin's orations and publications discussing the importance of colonists' rights to Washington's role as commander-in-chief of the colonial army, each wholly dedicated himself to the independence movement.

When protests and attempts at diplomacy failed to win the colonies what they needed, the colonists turned to their military to confront British forces head-on. Washington—who secured numerous American victories, including the decisive victory at Yorktown—and such generals as Horatio Gates and Nathanael Greene—who helped the colonies win pivotal battles at

Saratoga and in the South, respectively—were critical in turning the tide of war in the colonies' favor. The military success of the colonies also depended on the efforts of militias and leaders such as "the swamp fox," Francis Marion, whose skill in navigating the forests and swampy terrain around Charleston, S.C., led to the defeat of British troops in the area.

Colonists were not the only ones for whom independence was a rallying call. The cry for freedom echoed far and wide, drawing in some seemingly unexpected allies such as Thaddeus Kosciusko and Casimir Pulaski, both of whom fought for freedom in their native Poland before coming to the aid of colonial forces. The French fighters Lafayette and Rochambeau also responded to the cry by serving with Washington during the war.

Not to be forgotten are the many individuals who risked their lives away from the front lines. Crispus Attucks, presumed to be an escaped slave, was challenging the British presence in the colonies when he was shot and killed in the Boston Massacre. Women, though denied permission to fight, found other ways to assist in the Revolution. Lydia

Barrington Darragh and Sybil Ludington, for example, were each able to warn colonial forces of impending British attacks, thus averting possible disaster.

The struggle for independence was fought on many fronts—some agitators took up their pens, others took up arms, and still others simply did whatever was necessary to aid the cause. No matter how they chose to show their support, however, the individuals you will encounter in this volume—and the many other heroes who devoted themselves to the Revolution—shared a commitment to their land and represent some of the country's most impassioned patriots, for whom sacrifice came second only to justice and freedom.

CHAPTER 1

BENJAMIN FRANKLIN

Benjamin Franklin was a printer by trade, but he had many other talents as well. He was a diplomat, a scientist, an inventor, a philosopher, an educator, and a public servant.

In Europe, Franklin was the most famous American of the Revolutionary era. It was he who persuaded the English to repeal the hated Stamp Act. It was also he who convinced the French to aid in the American Revolution. Franklin helped draft both the Declaration of Independence and the U.S. Constitution.

EARLY LIFE

Benjamin Franklin was born in Boston on Jan. 17, 1706. His father, Josiah, was a poor soap- and candlemaker. His mother, Abiah, was Josiah's second wife. Benjamin was the youngest son and the 15th of 17 children. When he was 12 he went to work as an apprentice in the print shop of his half brother James. He soon became an expert printer, but he was not happy in his brother's shop and wanted to be on his own.

After a short stay in New York City, Franklin went to Philadelphia. In 1728 he started his own print shop with a partner, and the two published a weekly newspaper called the *Pennsylvania Gazette*. Franklin became sole owner of the business in 1730 and went on to become very successful. He was made official printer for Pennsylvania, New Jersey, Delaware, and Maryland. Franklin's most popular publication was *Poor Richard's Almanack*, which first appeared in 1732. The *Almanack* was a calendar and weather forecast for the year, and it contained amusing stories and proverbs.

At Franklin's insistence Philadelphia's streets were paved and kept clean and better lighted. He formed Philadelphia's first volunteer fire company. He used the editorial columns of the *Gazette* to raise money for organizing the first hospital in America. He started the first circulating library in America. He also helped establish an academy that later became the University of Pennsylvania.

By 1748 Franklin had earned enough money to leave his printing business. He bought a 300-acre (120-hectare) farm near Burlington, N.J., and retired to give his time to science and public service.

A cover page of Benjamin Franklin's popular publication **Poor Richard's Almanack,** *from 1739. Richard Saunders, the name shown, was one of Franklin's pen names and the character responsible for the Almanack's* **witty proverbs.** © **AP Images**

INVENTOR, SCIENTIST, AND PUBLIC SERVANT

Franklin was an active inventor all his adult life. The most famous of his many inventions included the Franklin stove, which was used to heat rooms, and bifocal eyeglasses. He was also recognized as one of the great scientific thinkers of the world. His contributions included pioneer studies of heat conduction and the origin of storms. His most important work, however, was done with electricity. He conducted many experiments and published a book that formed the basis for modern electrical theory.

Franklin also filled many public offices. He was a clerk of the Pennsylvania Assembly from 1736 to 1751 and a member of the Assembly from 1751 to 1764. He served as deputy postmaster of Philadelphia from 1737 to 1753, when he was made deputy postmaster general for all the colonies.

In 1757 Franklin was sent by the Pennsylvania Assembly to London to represent the colony in a tax dispute involving the Penn family, which governed the colony from England. For five years he stayed in England, meeting many people important in science and politics. He returned to Pennsylvania in

1762. Two years later, when another disagreement arose between Pennsylvania and the Penns, the Assembly sent Franklin back to England to propose that the colony be governed by the king rather than by the Penns.

REVOLUTIONARY ERA

In 1765, shortly after Franklin again landed in England, Parliament passed the Stamp Act, which taxed publications and legal documents throughout the colonies. Never before had England laid a direct tax upon the colonists without giving them a chance to vote on it in their assemblies. A fury of protest broke out, and Americans refused to buy the stamps required on the documents.

Franklin was called before the English House of Commons for questioning. He presented the American position so clearly and reasonably that Parliament was persuaded to repeal the Stamp Act. Franklin was hailed as a great statesman.

For the next 10 years Franklin was the most important American representative in England. He was made the London agent of several American colonies. Through talks and in pamphlets and newspaper articles, he tried to show that if the colonists were granted rights equal to those of English citizens, peace could be made. He became famous in Europe as a wit and a champion of liberty as well as a scientist. Many Englishmen in power, however, refused to listen to Franklin's good advice. Open rebellion broke out in America.

Franklin returned to Philadelphia in 1775, landing just after the battles of Lexington and Concord had been fought. Although Franklin was nearly 70 years old, he plunged into the work of the Revolution.

At once he was made the first postmaster general of the colonies and a member of the Second Continental Congress. In 1775 Congress appointed Franklin one of three men to go to George Washington's headquarters at Cambridge, Mass., to confer on problems of the Continental Army. He helped draft the Declaration of Independence and later the Articles of Confederation, which served as the first constitution of the United States.

In 1776 Congress sent Franklin on his most important diplomatic mission. He was asked to persuade France to help America in its fight for independence.

Franklin was very popular in Paris. He enjoyed the parties given in his honor and made many close friends among the French people.

From left to right, Benjamin Franklin, Thomas Jefferson, John Adams, Robert Livingston, and Roger Sherman. Franklin, along with his cohorts, helped draft the Declaration of Independence. **Stock Montage/Archive Photos/Getty Images**

He also worked very hard. First he had to secure formal recognition for his country. Then he had to persuade the French that an alliance would be helpful to them. He was successful, and the Treaty of Paris was signed Feb. 6, 1778.

Franklin remained in France as a representative of America. In 1781 he was named one of the commissioners to negotiate peace with Great Britain. When the Revolution was won, Franklin was one of the signers of the peace treaty.

LAST YEARS

Franklin returned to Philadelphia in 1785. Old and frail as he was, he became president of the Pennsylvania Assembly, a post equal to that of governor. He served in this post for three years. Franklin was also the oldest member of the Constitutional Convention, which wrote the U.S. Constitution.

Franklin spent the last five years of his life in Philadelphia. During this time he wrote newspaper articles and his famous autobiography. His final public act was to sign a memorial to the state legislature as president of the Pennsylvania Society for the Abolition of Slavery. Franklin died on April 17, 1790.

CHAPTER 2

JAMES OTIS

During the troubled days before the American Revolution, James Otis fought for the rights of the colonists. His pamphlets protested British violation of those rights. They were widely read in both America and England. He helped bring the colonies to their first united action in the Stamp Act Congress of 1765.

James Otis was born in West Barnstable, Mass., on Feb. 5, 1725. He was the eldest of the 13 children of Colonel James Otis, a lawyer, politician, and judge. The younger James attended Harvard College (now Harvard University), graduating in 1743. He then read law and was admitted to the bar in 1748. In 1750 he moved to Boston, and in the spring of 1755 he married Ruth Cunningham, the daughter of a wealthy Boston merchant. They had three children.

Otis was the king's advocate general in the vice admiralty court at Boston and as such was ordered to obtain court writs that would permit searching for smuggled goods without a search warrant. Rather than do this, Otis resigned and became the leader of the opposing counsel. In a dramatic four-hour speech at a court hearing

in 1761, he defended the Americans' rights to the protection against illegal search provided under English law.

Two months after the speech, Otis was elected to the Massachusetts legislature. He served until 1769 and with Samuel Adams shared the political leadership of Massachusetts.

Otis was an active member of the Sons of Liberty and other patriotic groups. In the legislature Otis made the motion that resulted in representatives of the American colonies meeting in New York City for the Stamp Act Congress of 1765.

In 1769 the king's customs commissioners in Boston described Otis as a "malignant incendiary" and accused him of treason. Otis retorted hotly in an article that appeared in the *Boston Gazette* of September 4. The next evening he entered a Boston coffeehouse where some commissioners were assembled. A brawl resulted, and Otis was struck on the head. He became insane, perhaps because of this blow.

Otis regained sanity for a time and in 1771 was again elected to the legislature. He soon exhibited new signs of derangement, however, and a court declared him insane. He was killed by a bolt of lightning on May 23, 1783, in Andover, Mass.

CHAPTER 3

PATRICK HENRY

Fearless and eloquent, Patrick Henry became the spokesman of the Southern colonies during the stirring period that led to the American Revolution. His words, which expressed the feelings and hopes of the patriots, helped inspire them to make those dreams into reality.

Patrick Henry was born on May 29, 1736, in Studley, Hanover County, Va. His mother was English. His father, an educated man who worked as a surveyor and county judge, was Scottish. Young Henry's formal education was scanty, and at the age of 15 he entered business. He failed as a farmer and as a storekeeper and turned his attention to the law. Admitted to the bar, he succeeded immediately as a pleader before frontier juries.

In 1763 Henry supported the people against the established church in a case known as the *Parson's Cause*. During the trial he declared in an impassioned speech that a king by vetoing acts of a colonial legislature "degenerates into a tyrant and forfeits all right to his subjects' obedience." This declaration brought him the love of the colonists and a seat in the Virginia

House of Burgesses just at the time of the passage of the Stamp Act in 1765.

The older members of the House hesitated, not knowing what course to take in regard to the Stamp Act. Henry introduced a series of resolutions declaring that the British Parliament had no right to tax the American colonies. In the debate that followed, Patrick Henry exclaimed: "Caesar had his Brutus; Charles the First, his Cromwell; and George the Third..." Here he was interrupted by loud cries of "Treason! Treason!" from members of the House. Henry paused for just a moment and then coolly finished: "and George the Third may profit by their example. If *this* be treason, make the most of it!" This fiery speech secured the adoption of the resolutions.

In 1774 Henry was sent by Virginia as a delegate to the First Continental Congress. At the second Virginia Convention the next year, he urged the colony to arm its militia. It was in this speech that he uttered the famous words:

> *Gentlemen may cry peace! peace! but there is no peace! The war is actually begun! The next gale that sweeps from the North will bring to our ears the clash of resounding arms! Our brethren are already in the field.*

Patrick Henry, left, speaks to the Virginia House of Burgesses in 1765 against the Stamp Act. **Fotosearch/Archive Photos/Getty Images**

Is life so dear, or peace so sweet as to be purchased at the price of chains and slavery? Forbid it, Almighty God! I know not what course others may take, but as for me, give me liberty, or give me death.

Henry also helped draw up Virginia's state constitution in 1776 and was elected first governor of the state. He was reelected twice.

In the Virginia ratification convention of 1788, Henry opposed the adoption of the new U.S. Constitution. He objected to it because it contained no "bill of rights" and because it infringed too much on the rights of the states. He wanted the country to remain a confederation and feared that under the Constitution it would become merely "one great consolidated national government of the people of all the States." Henry's advice to reject the Constitution was not followed, but it was as the result of such opposition that the first 10 amendments to the Constitution, popularly known as the Bill of Rights, were adopted.

Henry retired to Red Hill, his plantation near Brookneal, Va. In 1799 he consented to serve again in the Virginia legislative assembly, but on June 6, before he could take his seat, he died of cancer at Red Hill.

CHAPTER 4

A prominent statesman and patriot during the period of the American Revolution, John Dickinson served as a member of the Stamp Act Congress of 1765, the First and Second Continental Congresses of 1774 and 1775 to 1776, and the Constitutional Convention of 1787.

Dickinson was born on Nov. 8, 1732, in Talbot County, Md. After studying law in London, he conducted his own practice in Philadelphia from 1757 to 1760. From 1765 to 1775 he was one of the most productive writers against British colonial tax policies. His *Letters from a Farmer in Pennsylvania, to the Inhabitants of the British Colonies* made him famous. Published in 1767 and 1768, they opposed the Townshend Acts, which imposed import duties on the colonies. In the Second Continental Congress, he was a principal author of the *Declaration... Setting Forth the Causes and Necessity of Their Taking up Arms* (1775). He at first opposed the Declaration of

Independence but fought against the British during the Revolution. He helped draft the Articles of Confederation in 1776 and 1777.

After helping draft the U.S. Constitution in 1787, he supported the document in a series of letters signed "Fabius." Dickinson College at Carlisle, Pa., chartered in 1783, was named in his honor. He died in Wilmington, Del., on Feb. 14, 1808.

CHAPTER 5

CRISPUS ATTUCKS

The first American to die at the Boston Massacre, Crispus Attucks was probably an escaped slave. He became a powerful symbol as a martyr in the American colonists' struggle against the British.

Attucks's life prior to the day of his death is still shrouded in mystery. Nothing is known for certain, but historians generally agree that Attucks was of mixed ancestry, of both African and Natick Indian descent. It is also believed that Attucks was the runaway slave described in a notice that ran in the *Boston Gazette* in 1750. In the 20-year interval between his escape from slavery and his death at the hands of British soldiers, Attucks probably spent a good deal of time aboard whaling ships.

Attucks reappeared on March 5, 1770. Two British regiments had been stationed in Boston after colonists had protested new British taxes, and resentment had been building. Toward evening of that day, a crowd of colonists gathered and taunted a small group of British soldiers, some pelting the soldiers

Crispus Attucks. **Archive Photos/Getty Images**

with snowballs. Tension mounted rapidly. A group of men from the docks approached, carrying sticks, with Attucks in the lead. The outnumbered soldiers opened fire. The first to fall was Attucks, his chest pierced by two bullets, one of the first to die in the struggle against the British. Two other Americans were killed instantly and two more mortally wounded.

The bodies of Attucks and 17-year-old ship's mate James Caldwell, neither of whom lived in Boston, were carried to Faneuil Hall, where they lay in state until March 8. On the day of the funeral of Attucks and three others, shops closed, and thousands of residents followed the procession to the Granary burial ground, where the men were buried in a common grave. The event was a galvanizing one for the colonists chafing under British rule. Pamphleteers and propagandists quickly dubbed it a "massacre."

Attucks was the only victim of the Boston Massacre whose name was widely remembered. In 1888 the Crispus Attucks monument was unveiled in Boston.

As a lawyer in the American colonies, John Adams fought for independence from Great Britain. As a diplomat, he helped to secure the peace. His prominent role in the Revolutionary era led to his election as first vice president and second president of the United States.

EARLY LIFE

John Adams was born on Oct. 30, 1735, in Braintree (now Quincy), Mass. His parents, John and Susanna Boylston Adams, were descendants of the first generation of Puritan settlers in New England. The elder Adams was a farmer, businessman, lieutenant of a militia, and a deacon in Braintree's Congregational church.

Adams enrolled at Harvard College (now Harvard University) in Cambridge, Mass., in 1751. He graduated in 1755 and then taught grade school for three years in Worcester, Mass. During this period Adams developed an interest in law and studied in his spare time under one of Boston's most prominent lawyers.

Adams was admitted to the Massachusetts bar in 1758 and established his own law practice in Braintree. In 1764 he married Abigail Smith, a Congregational minister's daughter from Weymouth, Mass. The couple had four children.

REVOLUTIONARY ACTIVITIES

Adams' political career began in Boston in 1765 when he was appointed as a town attorney to challenge the legality of British taxation in the colonies. The British Parliament had instituted the Stamp Act in 1765, which levied a tax on all publications and legal documents in the colonies. The act enraged the colonists, inspiring riots and a boycott of goods that required stamped papers. The widespread protests coupled with the impassioned legal arguments of Adams and his colleagues forced Parliament to repeal the act in 1766. Adams also led the opposition against the Townshend Acts of 1767, which imposed taxes on imported British goods.

Although hostile toward the British government, Adams used his legal skills to defend British soldiers who killed five colonists in the Boston Massacre of 1770. He attested that the

34

crowd had provoked the soldiers by taunting and threatening them. Six of the eight British soldiers involved in the incident were acquitted. Adams' insistence on upholding the legal rights of the soldiers made him temporarily unpopular, but it also marked him as one of the most principled radicals in the growing movement for American independence.

CONTINENTAL CONGRESS

In 1774 Adams attended the First Continental Congress in Philadelphia as a Massachusetts delegate. Along with the other members, he rejected any further reconciliation with Great Britain. At the Second Continental Congress in 1775, soon after the outbreak of the American Revolution, Adams nominated George Washington as commander-in-chief of all colonial military forces.

Adams played a major role as the Congress debated independence. He selected Thomas Jefferson to draft the Declaration of Independence and demanded unanimous congressional support for it. On July 4, 1776, Adams and the rest of the Congress approved the Declaration. The Continental Congress then formulated a plan for a

From left to right, John Adams, Robert Morris, Alexander Hamilton, and Thomas Jefferson. Adams attended both the First and Second Continental Congresses. **Library of Congress Prints and Photographs Division**

national government with the Articles of Confederation.

In 1779 Adams participated in the Massachusetts Constitutional Convention. He composed the Massachusetts constitution in 1780; the new document authorized formation of a bicameral, or two-chambered,

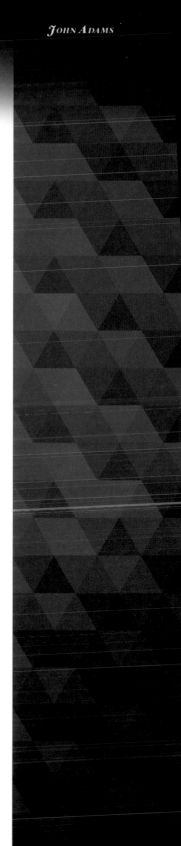

legislature and the separation of powers within the state government. The Massachusetts constitution provided a foundation for the constitutions of other states and later served as the model for the U.S. Constitution.

FOREIGN DIPLOMACY AND VICE PRESIDENCY

Beginning in 1778 Adams served for a decade as a diplomat in France, the Netherlands, and Great Britain. After the British surrendered to the United States in 1781, he joined Benjamin Franklin in Paris to negotiate a peace treaty. The Treaty of Paris, signed in 1783, officially ended the American Revolution. Adams and Franklin, experienced and shrewd foreign diplomats, were credited with achieving favorable terms in the treaty. In 1785 Adams was appointed the first U.S. ambassador to Great Britain.

Adams returned to the United States in 1788 and was placed on the ballot in the first presidential election in 1789. George Washington was elected president, and Adams became vice president. Adams' primary role as vice president was to cast the deciding vote in the Senate to break a tie.

PRESIDENCY

In the presidential election of 1796, Adams ran against Thomas Jefferson. Adams prevailed by a narrow margin of electoral votes. Jefferson became vice president.

When Adams began his presidency, the United States was involved in a naval conflict with France. French ships were attacking U.S. merchant vessels in the West Indies. In 1797 Adams sent three delegates to Paris to negotiate a peace settlement. Three French officials demanded a bribe before any talks could begin. Outraged by France's audacity, Adams ordered his delegates home and began preparing U.S. military forces for war with France. Adams referred to the three French officials as X, Y, and Z in his correspondence to Congress, and the incident became known as the XYZ Affair.

The XYZ Affair incited the Federalists in Congress to issue the Alien and Sedition Acts in 1798. Adams signed the acts into law. The acts permitted the government to deport foreign-born residents and indict anyone who published "false, scandalous, and malicious writing or writings against the government of the United States." By 1802,

however, these acts had been either repealed or allowed to expire. Their passage was Adams' chief domestic failure.

Adams and Thomas Jefferson ran against each other again in the presidential election of 1800. Jefferson won, and he succeeded Adams in 1801. Adams died in Quincy within hours of Jefferson's death on July 4, 1826, the 50th anniversary of the adoption of the Declaration of Independence.

CHAPTER 7

ABIGAIL ADAMS

A bigail Adams was the wife of John Adams, second president of the United States, and mother of John Quincy Adams, the sixth U.S. president. She was a prolific letter writer whose correspondence gives an intimate portrayal of life in the young republic.

Abigail Smith, the daughter of a Congregational minister, was born on Nov. 22 (Nov. 11 on the calendar used then), 1744, in Weymouth, Mass. She spent much of her childhood at the home of her grandparents in what is now Quincy, Mass., where—despite little formal education—she read widely in English, French, and history, and early displayed a lively intelligence. Her marriage on Oct. 25, 1764, to John Adams, a young Boston lawyer, began a lifetime partnership of support and mutual respect that many considered an ideal union. The couple had four children—Abigail, John Quincy, Charles, and Thomas.

For 10 years beginning in 1774, Adams was largely separated from her husband at the

Abigail Adams. **Stock Montage/Archive Photos/Getty Images**

family home in Quincy while he attended to federal business at the Continental Congress in Philadelphia. As the revolutionary spirit swept through the colonies, Abigail firmly supported the movement for independence. In March 1776, when her husband prepared to gather with his colleagues to write what would become the Declaration of Independence, she asked him to "remember the ladies and be more generous and favorable to them than your ancestors." Other letters also documented her strong views on the roles women should be allowed to play in society, and she is considered one of the first American feminists. She especially was interested in educational opportunities for women. Another issue of great concern to her was slavery, which she strongly opposed.

Following the peace treaty of 1783, Adams joined her husband abroad while he served in diplomatic posts in Paris, The Hague, and London. Her letters to friends and family at home again provide a colorful commentary on manners and customs.

During the 12-year period when John Adams served as vice president and president

of the United States, Abigail moved back and forth between Massachusetts and Philadelphia (the temporary capital)—once more filling in the absences with her flowing commentary. In November 1800 she oversaw the Adamses' move from Philadelphia to the newly constructed presidential mansion in Washington, D.C., soon to be called the White House. In 1801 the Adamses retired to Quincy, and Abigail died there on Oct. 28, 1818.

CHAPTER 8

SAMUEL ADAMS

A strong attachment to the cause of independence made Samuel Adams a leader of the American Revolution. He helped to start it and he helped to keep it going—by speeches, newspaper articles, and behind-the-scenes maneuvers. He combined great ideals with shrewd politics, and he worked hard to help America change from a British colony into an independent nation.

Samuel Adams was born Sept. 27, 1722, in Boston, Mass. His father was a well-to-do brewer and active in politics himself. Samuel was one of 12 children. As a boy, he attended Boston Grammar School, and in 1736 he entered Harvard College (now Harvard University). He graduated in 1740. Three years later he went back and studied for a Master of Arts degree. He was already thinking of revolution, for he chose as his thesis subject: "Whether it be lawful to resist the Supreme Magistrate, if the Commonwealth cannot otherwise be preserved."

Adams had little inclination for the brewery business he inherited from his father and ran into debt. His first wife died, leaving behind two children. His second wife practiced strict economy and gratefully accepted food and clothing from her neighbors. Adams devoted himself to public affairs. As a member of the Caucus, a political group that met in an attic, he learned the arts of the politician.

Adams' influence was due largely to his skill as a writer and to his passionate faith in the cause he served. In 1764 he was chosen to write Boston's protest against England's proposed Stamp Act. In 1765 he was elected to the Massachusetts colonial assembly and became the leader of opposition to the British government. In local politics he was called "the man of the town meeting." He brought about the creation in Boston in 1772 of a "committee of correspondence" to rouse public opinion. Adams' famous "circular letter" appealed to all the colonies to join in action against the crown. In 1773 Adams presided over the mass meeting that gave the signal for the Boston Tea Party.

As a delegate to the First and the Second Continental Congress, Adams fought for colonial independence. He signed the Declaration of Independence and, in 1788, secured the ratification of the Constitution by Massachusetts though he was at first opposed to the document. In 1794 he was elected governor of his state. He died on Oct. 2, 1803.

CHAPTER 9

PAUL REVERE

On the night of April 18, 1775, Paul Revere rode to warn American patriots northwest of Boston that the British intended to raid Lexington and Concord. The ride of this American Revolution folk hero was immortalized in Henry Wadsworth Longfellow's 1863 ballad, *Paul Revere's Ride*.

Revere was born on Jan. 1, 1735, in Boston, Mass. He was the third child of a silversmith, Apollos De Revoire. Apollos was a French Huguenot who had come to Boston as a boy. Later he changed his name to the simpler Revere. Young Revere became an excellent craftsman in fine metals. In 1757 he married Sarah Orne. When she died in 1773, Revere married Rachel Walker. He had eight children by each wife, but five of the children died in infancy. Revere was an early member of the Sons of Liberty, and he was one of the leaders of the Boston Tea Party in 1773.

When Revere set out on his famous journey to alert his countrymen, the redcoats were on the march primarily in search of Samuel Adams and John Hancock, who were in Lexington. Another British objective was

On his storied ride, Paul Revere alerts colonists to prepare for British raids on Lexington and Concord. **Time & Life Pictures/Getty Images**

to seize the store of patriot arms at Concord. As a result of Revere's warnings, the Lexington minutemen were ready the next morning for the arrival of the British and for the historic battle that launched the American Revolution.

During the war Revere engraved the printing plates for Massachusetts' first currency, set up a powder mill, and served in the local militia. In 1792 he opened a foundry to cast cannon and bells. He found a way to alloy copper and make brass. At 65 he became the first person in the United States to learn how to roll sheet copper. His copper sheets were used to resheathe the bottom of the *Constitution* ("Old Ironsides"). Revere died in Boston on May 10, 1818.

CHAPTER 10

THOMAS PAINE

Thomas Paine was the "firebrand of the American Revolution." His writings brought courage in times of crisis. The first was in January 1776. At that time the colonies were still split on the question of declaring their independence from Britain. Some instructed their delegates in the Continental Congress to act against separation from the mother country. Thousands of colonists were undecided. On January 10 Paine published a pamphlet, *Common Sense*. To rally the faltering he wrote: "Freedom has been hunted around the globe. Asia and Africa have expelled her...and England has given her warning to depart. O, receive the fugitive and prepare in time an asylum for mankind!" Colonists up and down the seaboard read this stirring call to action. George Washington himself said it turned doubt into decision—for independence.

Thomas Paine was born on Jan. 29, 1737, in Thetford, England. His mother was an Anglican; his father, a corset maker, was a Quaker. The family was poor, and at 13 years of age young Thomas left school to work for his father. At 19 he shipped out on a privateer in the Seven Years' War. In a few months, however,

COMMON SENSE;

ADDRESSED TO THE

INHABITANTS

OF

AMERICA,

On the following interesting

SUBJECTS.

I. Of the Origin and Design of Government in general, with concise Remarks on the English Constitution.

II. Of Monarchy and Hereditary Succession.

III. Thoughts on the present State of American Affairs.

IV. Of the present Ability of America, with some miscellaneous Reflections.

Man knows no Master save creating HEAVEN,
Or those whom choice and common good ordain.

THOMSON.

PHILADELPHIA;

Printed, and Sold, by R. BELL, in Third-Street.

M DCC LXX VI.

The cover of Thomas Paine's Common Sense. *The influential pamphlet sold more than 500,000 copies in just a few months.* **MPI/Archive Photos/Getty Images**

he left and became an apprentice to a London manufacturer. During the next few years he jumped from job to job, finally becoming a collector of excise taxes. Meanwhile he studied widely, especially in science and mechanics. He was dismissed from the excise office in 1772 after publishing an argument for a pay raise as the way to end corruption in the service.

Paine sailed for America, carrying letters of introduction from Benjamin Franklin, whom he had met in London. Franklin recommended him for the "genius in his eyes." Franklin's letters got him the post of assistant editor of the new *Pennsylvania Magazine* in Philadelphia. He also published articles and poetry anonymously or under pseudonyms. One essay denounced slavery in the colonies.

He served for a time in the Continental Army, sharing the hardships of the ill-equipped, hard-pressed American troops. He saw the mounting discouragement, and on Dec. 19, 1776, he started publishing *The Crisis*, a series of 16 pamphlets. It began with the challenging words: "These are the times that try men's souls." Washington ordered it read to "every corporal's guard in the army."

Paine was given a post by the Continental Congress. He published confidential information, however, and was forced to resign in 1779. He was then appointed clerk of Pennsylvania's General Assembly. He used part of his salary to start a subscription for the relief of soldiers. Although his pamphlets had sold well, he refused to accept the profits from his writings, and after the Revolution he was destitute. Congress buried his plea for assistance, but the states of New York and Pennsylvania granted him land and money.

Paine returned to England in 1787. There he published *Rights of Man* in 1791 in support of the French Revolution. Today the book seems moderate, but it so stirred Britain that he was indicted for treason. He fled to France and was elected to the National Convention. There he opposed the execution of Louis XVI. His humanitarian stand won him the ill will of the Jacobins, and he escaped the guillotine only through the fall of Maximilien Robespierre. After 10 months in prison he was released and aided by James Monroe, then U.S. ambassador to France and later president.

Paine's criticism of organized religion in *The Age of Reason* (1794, 1796) lost him many friends. He was not an atheist, however, but a deist. He returned to the United States in 1802. An outcast and in ill health, he wandered from place to place until his death on June 8, 1809, in New York City.

CHAPTER 11

THOMAS JEFFERSON

Thomas Jefferson was the chief author of the Declaration of Independence and the third president of the United States. His remarkable public career also included service in the Continental Congress, as the country's first secretary of state, and as its second vice president. Among the Founding Fathers, Jefferson was the most eloquent proponent of individual freedom as the core meaning of the American Revolution.

EARLY LIFE

Thomas Jefferson was born on April 13, 1743, in Shadwell, Va. His father, Peter Jefferson, was a landowner, surveyor, and public official. His mother, Jane Randolph Jefferson, was descended from one of the most prominent families in Virginia. In 1745 the family moved to Tuckahoe, the Randolph plantation near Richmond, Va. Thomas was educated by private tutors until 1752, when his family returned to Shadwell. He continued his education at boarding schools and the College of William and Mary in Williamsburg, Va., where he studied law for five years. He became a lawyer in 1767.

In 1768 Jefferson returned to Shadwell and built a mansion on an 867-foot (264-meter) mountain nearby. He named his new estate Monticello, an Italian word meaning "little mountain." On Jan. 1, 1772, Jefferson married Martha Wayles Skelton, a widow whose estate more than doubled Jefferson's land-holdings when the couple combined their properties. The couple had six children, but only two survived childhood.

Monticello, Thomas Jefferson's home. Shutterstock.com

Jefferson depended on slave labor for the upkeep of Monticello. His ownership of slaves would become perhaps the most controversial aspect of his legacy. Even as he maintained that slavery contradicted the principles of freedom and equality upon which the United States was founded, he insisted that it was wrong for the federal government to end the practice. Further complicating the issue is Jefferson's relationship with Sally Hemings, one of his house slaves. In 1998 DNA evidence revealed that Jefferson almost certainly fathered at least one child with Hemings.

DECLARATION OF INDEPENDENCE

In 1769 Jefferson was elected to the House of Burgesses, Virginia's representative assembly. He used his law knowledge to support colonial opposition to British legislation and taxation. In 1774 Jefferson wrote the influential essay *A Summary View of the Rights of British America*, which stated that the British Parliament had no authority to legislate for the colonies. After the American Revolution began in 1775, the Virginia legislature appointed Jefferson as a delegate to the Second Continental Congress in Philadelphia. The Congress called for independence from Great Britain.

In 1776 Jefferson was selected to a committee to outline a formal document outlining the reasons for independence. The committee, which also included John Adams and Benjamin Franklin, chose Jefferson to draft the document. He expressed what

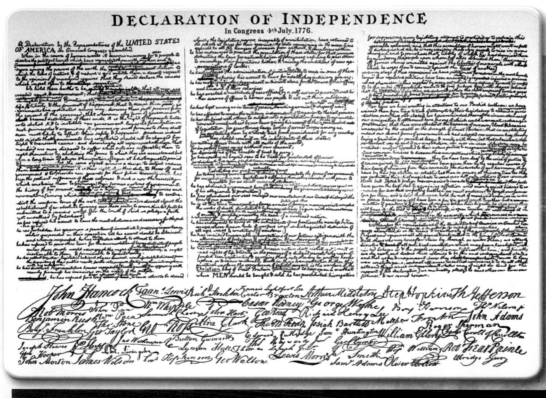

Thomas Jefferson's draft of the Declaration of Independence. Time & Life Pictures/Getty Images

the majority of the colonists desired when he wrote: "We hold these truths to be self-evident, that all men are created equal, that they are endowed by their Creator with certain unalienable Rights, that among these are Life, Liberty, and the pursuit of Happiness...." On July 4, 1776, the Continental Congress adopted the Declaration of Independence, which officially announced the separation of the colonies from Great Britain.

STATE AND NATIONAL POLITICS

Jefferson retired from the Continental Congress in 1776 and returned to the Virginia legislature. With the assistance of James Madison, Jefferson drafted the Virginia constitution complete with a declaration of rights. The Virginia constitution served as a model for the U.S. Constitution. As a law-maker he proposed bills to end the privileges of the wealthy, to make education available to everyone, and to separate church and state.

Jefferson was elected governor of Virginia in 1779. The American Revolution reached Virginia in 1780 as British troops invaded Richmond. Jefferson's administration retreated from the capital while he assembled his family at Monticello. The Virginia press labeled him a coward for abandoning his duties as governor. In 1781 he retired from public life and returned to Monticello. His retirement was short-lived, however, as he returned to the Continental Congress in 1782.

After the American Revolution ended, the Continental Congress sent Jefferson to Paris to succeed Benjamin Franklin as U.S. ambassador to France. The U.S. Constitution was ratified while Jefferson was in Paris. When he returned to the United States in 1789, Jefferson criticized the framers of the Constitution for its lack of a bill of rights. He argued that every U.S. citizen was entitled to rights provided by the national government. He also asserted that the authority of the federal government under the Constitution severely imposed on states' rights.

After George Washington became the first president of the United States in 1789, he appointed Jefferson as U.S. secretary of state. However, frustrated by political differences within the administration, Jefferson

retired from the post in 1793 and returned to Monticello. He reentered national politics with a run for the presidency in 1796. He was defeated by John Adams in a closely contested race. Under the system of the time, Jefferson became vice president.

PRESIDENCY

In 1800 Jefferson ran for president again. This time he tied Aaron Burr with 73 electoral votes. The decision was thrown to the U.S. House of Representatives, which chose Jefferson after more than 30 ballots. As president, Jefferson reduced the authority of the U.S. government by dismantling the military, lowering taxes, and decreasing the national debt. He also dispensed with much of the ceremony and formality that had attended the office of president to that time.

In 1803 Jefferson oversaw the Louisiana Purchase, in which the United States acquired the vast Louisiana Territory from France. It doubled the land area of the country. Soon afterward Jefferson sent Meriwether Lewis and William Clark to explore the Louisiana Territory. Their expedition paved the way for future explorers and traders who sought to colonize the West.

When war resumed between Great Britain and France in 1803, Jefferson insisted that the United States remain neutral. However, both European countries distrusted the United States and seized U.S. merchant vessels that were suspected of carrying war supplies. In response to the harassment, Jefferson signed the Embargo Act in 1807, which closed all U.S. ports to import and export shipping. Jefferson theorized that restricting trade with the United States would convince Great Britain and France to honor U.S. neutrality. Instead, the Embargo Act backfired and wrecked the U.S. economy.

Jefferson left office in 1809. In retirement, he planned the layout and designed the buildings of the University of Virginia in Charlottesville. Jefferson and John Adams died within hours of each other on July 4, 1826 — the 50th anniversary of the adoption of the Declaration of Independence.

CHAPTER 12

JOHN HANCOCK

The man whose name heads the list of signers of the Declaration of Independence, John Hancock was a Boston patriot and a leader of the American Revolution. His prominent signature is familiar to anyone who has seen a picture of that document.

John Hancock was born on Jan. 12, 1737, in Braintree, Mass. His father died when John was a child, and he was adopted by his uncle, a rich Boston merchant. Hancock inherited his uncle's wealth when he was 28 years old. In 1768 his ship, *Liberty*, was seized by British authorities for nonpayment of duty. Its cargo of wine had been smuggled ashore. The seizure precipitated a riot on shore. The British used the ship as a coast guard vessel until it was burned by a patriot mob in Newport, R.I.

The episode was a prelude to the Revolution. Hancock's opposition to British rule was no doubt inspired by business interest, but, whatever his motives, he was valuable to the cause. In 1770, after the Boston Massacre, he was one of the committee that

John Hancock's famed signature can be seen on this copy of the *Declaration of Independence.* Todd Gipstein/National Geographic Image Collection/Getty Images

went to the governor to demand the removal of British troops from the city. At the funeral of the victims he delivered an address that led to an order for his arrest. He presided at the revolutionary Provincial Congress that met in Concord and later in Cambridge, and his arrest was one of the objects of the British expedition to Concord. This expedition led to the battles of Lexington and Concord.

Elected president of the Second Continental Congress in 1775, Hancock held that office for two years. In 1780 he became the first elected governor of Massachusetts and, except for two years (1785–87), he held that office until his death. The support he was persuaded to give to the U.S. Constitution in 1788 was the decisive factor in its struggle for ratification in Massachusetts.

Hancock was a man of strong common sense and sound patriotism. His wealth, social position, and education were of great help to the colonial cause. He died on Oct. 8, 1793, in Quincy, Mass.

CHAPTER 13

On June 7, 1776, Richard Henry Lee offered the resolution in the U.S. Congress "that these colonies are, and of right ought to be, free and independent states." Lee's fame rests on this history-making resolution, but he served his country in many other ways.

Richard Henry Lee was born on Jan. 20, 1732, in Virginia. At 25 he took a seat in the Virginia House of Burgesses. He was among the first to suggest that the colonists organize committees to achieve unified action against the British. Lee was a signer of the Declaration of Independence and president of the Continental Congress from 1784 to 1786.

Lee was opposed to the idea of a constitution. He and Patrick Henry were its most violent critics. They feared that it would deprive the states of their rights and might become an instrument of tyranny. In 1789 he accepted appointment as senator from Virginia. In the Senate Lee became one of the strongest advocates of the first 10 amendments, the Bill of Rights. Ill health forced him to retire in 1792. He died on June 19, 1794, in Westmoreland County, Va.

Remembered as the Father of His Country, George Washington stands alone in American history. He was commander-in-chief of the Continental Army during the American Revolution, chairman of the convention that wrote the U.S. Constitution, and the first president of the United States. His ideals of liberty and democracy set a standard for future presidents and for the entire country.

EARLY LIFE

The eldest child of Augustine and Mary Ball Washington, George Washington was born on Feb. 22, 1732, on the Wakefield plantation in Westmoreland County, Va. His father was a prosperous landowner who managed farms, businesses, and mines. Later the family moved to Ferry Farm on the Rappahannock River, opposite Fredericksburg, Va.

After his father's death in 1743, George lived at Wakefield and attended Henry William's school, one of the best schools in Virginia. By age 15 he was skilled in

George Washington. SuperStock/Getty Images

mathematics and mapmaking and had developed an interest in surveying.

In 1748 George went to live with his half brother Lawrence at an estate on the Potomac River named Mount Vernon. There he met a wealthy landowner who hired him to help survey his holdings in Virginia. George excelled at his new profession. In July 1749 he was appointed surveyor of Culpeper County, his first public office. When Lawrence died in 1752, George inherited Mount Vernon, thus becoming a landowner.

Inspired by his brother's experiences in the British Navy, Washington pursued a military career. Beginning in 1754 he fought in the French and Indian War, a conflict between the British and the French over control of the Ohio River Valley. Washington led his troops and their Native American allies against the French at Fort Duquesne, at the site of present-day Pittsburgh, Pa. In 1755, after British Gen. Edward Braddock was killed, Washington was appointed commander of all Virginia's troops. In 1758 he accompanied British Gen. John Forbes and finally defeated the French at Fort Duquesne. Washington resigned from the army with the honorary rank of brigadier general.

Entry into Politics

While serving in the final campaign against Fort Duquesne, Washington was elected to the Virginia House of Burgesses. In 1759 he married a young widow, Martha Dandridge Custis. From the time of his marriage, Washington supervised both Mount Vernon and the large Custis estate, thus becoming one of the wealthiest and most industrious landowners in Virginia.

Washington's happy life was interrupted by deteriorating relations between Great Britain and the colonies. After the French and Indian War ended in 1763, Britain faced a heavy debt as well as continued military costs to protect the land it acquired during the war. As the British government imposed new taxes to generate revenue from the colonies, the colonists protested. Some demanded independence at once.

A loyal British subject, Washington was not yet in favor of separation from Great Britain. However, he believed that the British had attacked the rights of the colonists, and he was ready to defend these rights. By the late 1760s he was calling for boycotts of British-made goods. In 1774 Washington and other Virginia legislators signed the resolutions calling for a Continental Congress. He was elected to the Virginia delegation that attended the First Continental Congress in Philadelphia on Sept. 5, 1774. He also attended the Second Continental Congress in 1775.

AMERICAN REVOLUTION

In April 1775 skirmishes between British troops and the colonists at Lexington and Concord intensified colonial hostility toward Great Britain. Though still not in favor of independence, Washington was prepared to support armed resistance against the British.

Recognizing Washington's military experience and leadership, the Continental Congress made him commander-in-chief of all colonial military forces in June 1775. Reports of how courageously the colonial militia fought against British soldiers at Bunker Hill in June 1775 gave Washington confidence about the impending war. However, he faced a multitude of hardships as he assembled the Continental Army. His recruits were untrained and poorly paid, terms of army enlistment were short, and his officers frequently quarreled among themselves.

Washington commanded the respect of his troops through his confidence, poise, and determination as a general. In March 1776 his army staged a siege and eventually expelled British troops from Boston. Washington also instilled a sense of national pride in his troops. He maintained discipline within his army by punishing dishonest soldiers and deserters. At the same time, he attended to their welfare by petitioning to the Continental Congress for better rations and pay.

On July 4, 1776, the Continental Congress adopted the Declaration of Independence. Congress wrote the Articles of Confederation, the first constitution in the United States, to implement a national government.

In December 1776 Washington's forces crossed the Delaware River from Pennsylvania to New Jersey and won battles at Trenton and Princeton. The Continental Army gained an advantage in the war with Gen. Horatio Gates's victory in New York at the Battle of Saratoga in October 1777. However, Washington's army suffered losses against the British forces in Pennsylvania at the battles of Brandywine and Germantown in the fall of 1777. In December 1777 Washington withdrew to Valley Forge, Pa., where he set up winter quarters. Enduring months of bitter cold and some 2,000 desertions, Washington managed to reorganize his army for the ongoing fight.

The decisive stroke of the war came under Washington's leadership in 1781. His army, with the help of French allies, staged a siege at Yorktown, Va. The commander of the British Army, Gen. Charles Cornwallis, was forced to

George Washington rides among his troops at Valley Forge, Pa. Washington's strong leadership held his army together in the face of harsh winter conditions and desertions. **Library of Congress Prints and Photographs Division**

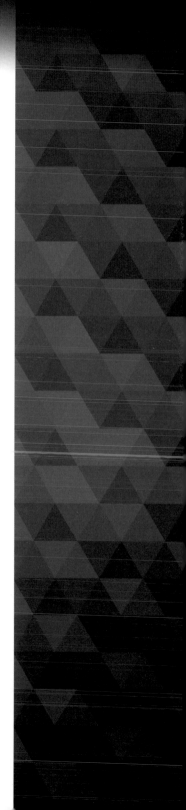

surrender. The Treaty of Paris was signed on Sept. 3, 1783, officially ending the American Revolution. Washington remained with the Continental Congress until December 1783, when he resigned his commission and returned to his home at Mount Vernon.

Washington's retreat to private life did not last long, however. Concerned with the chaotic political situation of the young country, Washington became a leader in the movement that led to the Constitutional Convention of 1787. For four months he presided over the convention as it drafted a new constitution to replace the ineffective Articles of Confederation.

PRESIDENCY

In 1789 the electoral college unanimously chose George Washington as the first president of the United States. He was elected to a second term in 1792. John Adams was his vice president.

Washington was committed to a strong federal government. He also believed that the United States should remain neutral in foreign affairs. When war broke out between France and Great Britain in 1793, Washington

decided that the United States should not interfere because the United States was not prepared to enter another war so soon. Accordingly, he issued the Proclamation of Neutrality, which stated that the United States must maintain a sense of national identity, independent from any other country's influence. Washington's successors continued his neutrality policy.

The U.S. government met its first serious domestic challenge with the Whiskey Rebellion in 1794. Washington set a tax on whiskey to help pay down the national debt. Farmers in western Pennsylvania who relied on income from selling whiskey resisted the tax by assaulting federal revenue officers. After negotiations failed, Washington dispatched 13,000 federal troops to quell the rebellion. The event reinforced the authority of the federal government.

When Washington's second term ended in 1796, he refused to run for a third. He considered it unwise for one person to hold such a powerful position for so long. The precedent he set was maintained until the 20th century, when Franklin D. Roosevelt served four terms as president. Washington retired to Mount Vernon, where he died on Dec. 14, 1799.

Until the arrival of George Washington, Gen. Artemas Ward served as chief commander at the 1775 siege of Boston during the American Revolution. He later served in the Continental Congress and the U.S. House of Representatives.

Ward was born on Nov. 26, 1727, in Shrewsbury, Mass., a city that his father, Nahum Ward, helped found. After graduating from Harvard College in 1748, he taught for a time and then established a general store. He held many town offices before being appointed a justice of the Worcester County court of common pleas in 1762; he later became its chief justice.

Ward gained a reputation as a champion for colonial rights, especially after organizing opposition to British general Thomas Gage's governorship of Massachusetts in the mid-1770s. Despite being ill, Ward (who had gained military experience in the provincial militia during the French and Indian War) immediately assumed command of the colonial troops in the American Revolution when

he heard about the Battle of Lexington in April 1775. In May he was formally commissioned general and commander-in-chief of the Massachusetts troops.

After Washington's arrival, Ward remained second in command as a major general. Before he had to resign because of his health, Ward was instrumental in seizing Dorchester Heights in March 1776 to force a British evacuation of Boston. His service actually lasted beyond his resignation because he honored Washington's request that he continue to command the forces left in Massachusetts after the withdrawal of the main body to New York.

Ward was president of the Massachusetts Executive Council (1777–79) before becoming a member (and later speaker) of his state's house of representatives (1779–85). From 1780 to 1782 he also served in the Continental Congress. During his term in the U.S. Congress, from 1791 to 1795, he participated on many committees dealing with military affairs. He died in Shrewsbury on Oct. 28, 1800.

CHAPTER 16

HORATIO GATES

General Horatio Gates won a decisive victory in 1777 against the British at Saratoga, N.Y., that turned the tide for the Continental Army in the American Revolution. However, his reputation became blemished when he was accused of conspiring to overthrow Gen. George Washington as commander-in-chief of the colonial forces.

Horatio Gates was born in about 1728 in Maldon, Essex County, England. He began his military career in North America as a captain in the British Army during the French and Indian War. Promoted during the war, he returned to England as a major in 1765. He retired from the British Army in 1769.

Financial difficulties caused Gates to seek new opportunities in North America. In 1772 he immigrated with his family to Berkeley County, Va. (now part of West Virginia). He soon adopted the colonial anti-British sentiment in the years preceding the American Revolution.

After the skirmishes at Lexington and Concord in 1775, Gates was commissioned

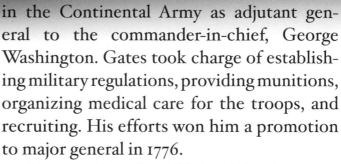

in the Continental Army as adjutant general to the commander-in-chief, George Washington. Gates took charge of establishing military regulations, providing munitions, organizing medical care for the troops, and recruiting. His efforts won him a promotion to major general in 1776.

In 1777, after Gen. Philip Schuyler experienced a series of defeats, Gates replaced him as commander of the Continental Army in the North. In the fall of that year Gates engaged British Gen. John Burgoyne in the two battles of Saratoga. With the help of Gen. Benedict Arnold in the second battle, Gates stopped Burgoyne's advance and forced him to surrender.

Gates became a hero after his triumph at Saratoga, and the Continental Congress named him president of the Board of War. At the time of his appointment, a group of army officers led by Gen. Thomas Conway publicly criticized George Washington's leadership in the war. In what became known as the "Conway Cabal," this group plotted to replace Washington with Gates as commander-in-chief of the Continental Army. The conspiracy quickly dissolved. Gates

General John Burgoyne of the British Army surrenders his sword to Gen. Horatio Gates after being defeated by him at Saratoga. **Three Lions/Hulton Archive/Getty Images**

and Washington made amends, but the trust between the generals had been broken.

Gates returned to his command in New York in the spring of 1778 and was reassigned to the South in 1780. He arrived in South Carolina to command a weakened army that had suffered a demoralizing loss to the British at Charleston in May 1780. Rather than reorganize and rest his weary troops, he

decided to march them toward the British at Camden. To Gates's surprise, British Gen. Charles Cornwallis had arrived recently at Camden to reinforce the British regiment there. Gates experienced a devastating defeat and was chastised by his superiors for careless planning and reckless errors.

The Continental Congress led an investigation into Gates's conduct at Camden, but charges against him were dropped. In 1783 Gates retired from the military and moved to New York, where he served one term in the state legislature. He died on April 10, 1806.

CHAPTER 17

FREDERICK WILLIAM STEUBEN

During the dark days of Valley Forge during the American Revolution, Frederick William Steuben, baron von Steuben, turned George Washington's corps of raw recruits into an efficient, well-trained army. He formed and commanded a model drill company that was copied throughout the ranks, and he was appointed inspector general in 1778.

Frederick William Steuben was born on Sept. 17, 1730, in Magdeburg, Prussia (now in Germany). He began his military career as an officer in the Prussian army when he was only 17. He served in the Seven Years' War as an infantry officer and then as a general staff officer until his discharge in 1763. In Paris in 1777 he received a letter of introduction to General Washington from Benjamin Franklin.

The impression Steuben made on the Continental Army was great. The general compiled the drill and field service regulations manual, even though he knew no

English. He was given a field command and participated in the siege of Yorktown in 1781. After the war he spent the rest of his life in America, becoming a citizen in 1783. New York gave him a grant of land in the central part of the state, and Congress granted him an annual pension of $2,800. He died on Nov. 28, 1794, at his New York estate.

CHAPTER 18

PHILIP JOHN SCHUYLER

As a soldier and a statesman, Philip John Schuyler helped make early American history. He aided in freeing the American colonies from British rule and in starting them on the road to becoming a nation.

Schuyler was born on Nov. 11, 1733, in Albany, N.Y. He was the oldest of four children. His ancestors were Dutch. His father was a merchant, alderman, and Indian commissioner. Taught by a clergyman in New Rochelle, N.Y., young Schuyler excelled in mathematics, surveying, and astronomy. In the 1750s he served the British as a supply officer in the French and Indian War.

General George Washington appointed Schuyler major general in 1775. Schuyler commanded the northern department in the American Revolution. For the most part he was a good officer, but he was criticized in 1777 for his loss of Fort Ticonderoga. Court-martialed in 1778 at his own request,

Philip John Schuyler. **MPI/Archive Photos/Getty Images**

he was acquitted with honor. He resigned from the Army the following year.

Schuyler served in Congress and on government boards and committees for many years. He was one of the first two U.S. senators from New York. He died in Albany on Nov. 18, 1804.

CHAPTER 19

BENEDICT ARNOLD

The name Benedict Arnold has become a synonym for a traitor to one's country. In the first years of the American Revolution, however, Arnold was a brilliant and dashing general, highly respected for his service to the patriot cause.

Benedict Arnold was born on Jan. 14, 1741, in Norwich, Conn. His father, Benedict, was a well-to-do landowner. His mother was Hannah King Waterman Arnold. While a boy, young Arnold twice ran away to join the colonial troops fighting in the French and Indian War. When he was 21 he settled in New Haven. In time he became a prosperous merchant and a captain in the Connecticut militia. He married Margaret Mansfield in 1767. They had three sons.

Arnold played a gallant part in the American Revolution and became a major general in 1777. His wife had died in 1775. Early in 1779 he married Margaret Shippen, by whom he had four sons and one daughter. Arnold lived lavishly and soon found himself badly pressed for money.

Benedict Arnold. **Interim Archives/Archive Photos/Getty Images**

He then began his treasonable activities. Most historians agree that Arnold did so for money, though he may also have resented lack of further promotion. Whatever his motive, he regularly sent vital military information to the British and was well paid for it. His wife helped him, often acting as messenger. In 1780 Arnold obtained command of West Point and at once conspired to turn over the garrison to the British. He met Maj. John André, a British spy, and made final plans. André was captured, however, and his papers indicated Arnold's treason.

Arnold heard of the capture and fled to the British headquarters in New York City. He was given a command and about £6,300. He served with the British for the rest of the war, leading troops on raids in Virginia and Connecticut. After the war he lived with his family in England. He failed to obtain a regular commission in the British Army and failed also in several business ventures, including land speculation in Canada. He died in London on June 14, 1801.

CHAPTER 20

NATHANAEL GREENE

As a general in the American Revolution, Nathanael Greene is often regarded as second only to George Washington. Because of his brilliant wartime strategy, he was called "the man who saved the South" from the British.

Nathanael Greene was born in Potowomut, R.I., on Aug. 7, 1742. His father, a blacksmith and a Quaker preacher, trained him in the strict principles of the Quakers. When Greene joined the militia, he was excommunicated by his church, which does not believe in warfare. His military training won him the command of the Rhode Island forces in 1775. He marched his troops to Cambridge after the skirmishes at Lexington and Concord and served with distinction at Trenton, Princeton, and Brandywine. At Washington's request, in March 1778 at Valley Forge he accepted the difficult position of quartermaster general, retaining, however, the right to command troops in the field.

Nathanael Greene. **MPI/Archive Photos/Getty Images**

Because of the meddling of Congress with the affairs of his department, Greene resigned his position in 1780. Shortly afterward Washington appointed him commander of the Army of the South. Greene found the army without discipline, arms, or clothing. He could not bring it into condition for fighting until 1781. As soon as this had been accomplished, he began a campaign that in less than a year stripped the English of all their conquests in the Carolinas and Georgia except Charleston, in which he confined the British Army for the rest of the war. For this he received the thanks of Congress and large grants of land. Greene settled on an estate near Savannah, Ga. He died on June 19, 1786.

CHAPTER 21

THADDEUS KOSCIUSKO

The Polish general Thaddeus Kosciusko fought for freedom on two continents. In 1776 he came to America from Warsaw to serve in the American Revolution. Later he defended his native land, though he was by then a U.S. citizen.

Kosciusko was born on Feb. 4, 1746, in Mereczowszczyzna in the Kingdom of Poland (now in Belarus). He was educated at the Piarist college in Lubieszów and the military academy in Warsaw, where he later served as an instructor.

In 1776 Kosciusko traveled to America and joined the colonial forces against the British. That August he was transferred to the Pennsylvania Committee of Defense in Philadelphia, where he took part in planning fortifications to defend the residence of the Continental Congress. For this work he was given the rank of engineer colonel. In spring 1777 he was assigned to the army of Gen. Horatio Gates at Fort Ticonderoga, in northern New York. Beginning in July Kosciusko became active in Gates's army, closing by

Thaddeus Kosciusko. **The Bridgeman Art Library/Getty Images**

fortifications all roads along the Hudson River and thus contributing to the surrender of the British Army under Gen. John Burgoyne at Saratoga on October 17. He spent the next two years fortifying West Point, N.Y., where in March 1780 he was appointed chief of the engineering corps. That summer, serving under Gen. Nathanael Greene in North Carolina, he twice rescued the army from enemy advances by directing the crossing of the Yadkin and Dan rivers. At the end of the war he was given U.S. citizenship and was made a brigadier general in the U.S. Army.

Poland meanwhile was suffering from external aggression and internal anarchy. Kosciusko returned to fight valiantly but unsuccessfully at Dubienka and elsewhere in 1792 against a Russian invasion. In 1794 he became dictator and commander-in-chief of Poland and successfully defended Warsaw against siege by Russian and Prussian armies. On Oct. 10, 1794, his army of 7,000 Poles was defeated by 16,000 Russians at Maciejowice, where he was wounded.

Kosciusko was released from a Russian prison in 1796. He revisited America, living for a time in Philadelphia. He died in Switzerland on Oct. 15, 1817.

CHAPTER 22

ETHAN ALLEN

One of the first heroes of the American Revolution was Ethan Allen. He was especially famed for leading a small force against the British at Fort Ticonderoga and winning a bloodless surrender on May 10, 1775.

Ethan Allen was born in Litchfield, Conn., on Jan. 21, 1738. In 1757 he served in the French and Indian War, at Fort William Henry on the New York frontier. In 1762 Allen married, and soon after he moved to the New Hampshire Grants (now Vermont) and bought farmland. Both New York and New Hampshire claimed this area under their colonial grants. Allen was a leader among the New Hampshire claimants, and in 1770 he was made the head of an irregular force that was called the Green Mountain Boys. Their attacks upon the Yorkers led the New York governor to offer a reward of £100 (about $485) for Allen's capture.

When the American Revolution started, Allen and members of the Connecticut assembly raised a small force. He led this band

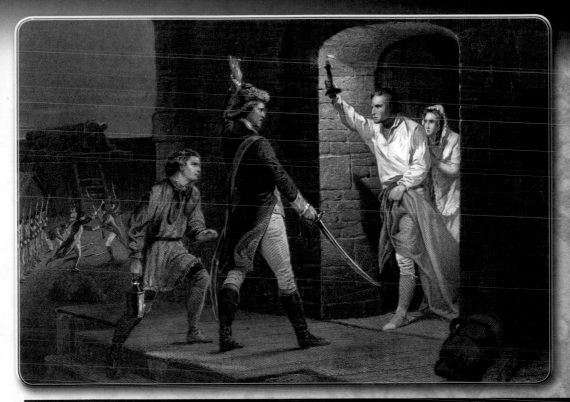

Ethan Allen's surprise attack on Fort Ticonderoga with his Green Mountain Boys led to British surrender of the fort. **Stock Montage/ Archive Photos/Getty Images**

and his Green Mountain Boys against Fort Ticonderoga. They arrived at dawn, and the astonished British commander surrendered. In the autumn Allen was captured while attacking Montreal. In 1778 an exchange of prisoners between the British and Americans brought Allen's release.

During this time the Hampshire Grant settlers had organized a provisional government and asked Congress for statehood. This government made Allen a major general. After they failed to win statehood, Allen plotted with the British to make Vermont a separate British province. For his part in this affair, he was accused of treason, but later the charge was dropped. Allen died in Burlington, Vt., on Feb. 12, 1789.

CHAPTER 23

Captured by the British and condemned to hang as a spy during the American Revolution, Nathan Hale said, "I only regret that I have but one life to lose for my country." Hale's words still stand as a lasting testimony to patriotism and courage.

Nathan Hale was born in Coventry, Conn., on June 6, 1755, the son of a prosperous farmer. He studied under a village minister and then entered Yale College in 1769. There he played sports, joined a literary fraternity, and talked about politics. One of the plays he probably read at Yale was Joseph Addison's *Cato*— Hale's last words paraphrased a speech made by a character in that tragedy. Hale graduated in 1773 and taught school in East Haddam, Conn., and then, a year later, in New London, Conn. People admired his learning and athletic prowess and the way he maintained discipline without severity.

When news of the British-American clash in Lexington, Mass., arrived at New London, Hale enlisted in the patriots' army. Commissioned a first lieutenant on July 1,

1775, he fought in Boston, Mass., and was promoted to captain on Jan. 1, 1776. In March the British evacuated Boston, and George Washington moved his army to New York City. Washington was defeated in the Battle of Long Island in August. He needed to know the British plans, and Hale undertook the dangerous spy mission. Dressed as a civilian, he crossed to Long Island from Norwalk, Conn., where he secured the information.

Nathan Hale stands among British soldiers before he is hanged. **MPI/ Archive Photos/Getty Images**

On the night of September 21 Hale was captured by the British as he tried to return to the American lines. Taken before Gen. William Howe and faced with the notes and maps that had been found concealed on his person, he admitted his rank and purpose. Howe ordered his execution. At 11:00 AM on Sept. 22, 1776, Hale mounted the gallows, uttered his famous words, and was hanged.

CHAPTER 24

Lydia Barrington Darragh was a heroine of the American Revolution. She is said to have saved Gen. George Washington's army from a British attack.

Lydia Barrington was born in Dublin, Ireland, in 1729. In 1753 she married William Darragh, a teacher. Shortly thereafter she immigrated with her husband to America, settling in Philadelphia. She worked as a nurse and midwife with considerable skill and success.

The event for which Darragh is remembered was told in a story first published in 1827 and later elaborated upon. During the British occupation of Philadelphia, British Gen. William Howe had his headquarters opposite the Darragh house. On the night of Dec. 2, 1777, the adjutant general and other officers commandeered one of her rooms for a secret conference, and, listening at the keyhole, she learned of their plan to attack Washington at Whitemarsh, 8 miles (13 kilometers) away, two nights later. On the morning of the day, December 4, she let it be known that she needed flour from the Frankford mill and obtained a pass to leave the city for that purpose. Once away, she made for Whitemarsh. Encountering Col. Thomas Craig, a friend, on the road, she told him what she had learned and then, securing her flour, hurried home. The British march that night found the Continental Army at arms and ready to repel, and Howe was forced to return to Philadelphia. Darragh lived in Philadelphia until her death, on Dec. 28, 1789.

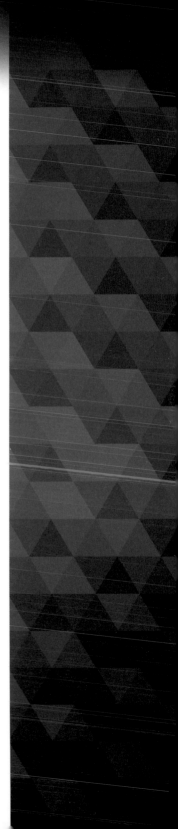

CHAPTER 25

SYBIL LUDINGTON

As a girl of only 16, Sybil Ludington made a valiant ride to spread the word of an impending British attack during the American Revolution. Her hometown in New York was renamed in her honor.

Ludington was born on April 5, 1761, in Fredericksburg (now Ludingtonville), N.Y. She was the daughter of Henry Ludington, a New York militia officer and later an aide to Gen. George Washington. On April 26, 1777, a messenger reached the Ludington house with news of Gov. William Tryon's attack on Danbury, Conn., some 15 miles (25 kilometers) to the southeast. The munitions and stores for the militia of the entire region were stored there. Colonel Ludington began immediately to organize the local militia. The messenger and his horse being exhausted, Sybil volunteered to rouse the countryside for the fight. Through the night the 16-year-old girl rode her horse nearly 40 miles (65 kilometers) on unfamiliar roads around Putnam County, spreading the alarm. She is believed to have covered twice the distance Paul Revere did on his famous ride in 1775. In 1784 Sybil married Edward Ogden, a lawyer, and she lived in Unadilla, N.Y., until her death. She died on Feb. 26, 1839.

Sybil Ludington rides around Putnam County, alerting the local militia of a planned British attack. Louis S. Glanzman/National Geographic Image Collection/Getty Images

CHAPTER 26

JOHANN KALB

When only 16 years old, ambitious Johann Kalb left his peasant home in Germany to find adventure. Some time later he embarked on a military career that would bring him to America to fight with the Continental Army in the Revolution.

Johann Kalb was born on June 29, 1721, in Hüttendorf (now in Germany). In 1743 he turned up in the French army as "Jean de Kalb," with the assumed title of "baron." Young "Baron de Kalb" rose swiftly to the rank of brigadier general. In 1767 the French government sent him to America to investigate secretly the possibilities of a revolt by the American colonies against England. They were not yet ready. Later, when they did rebel, he offered his services. With his protégé, the young Marquis de Lafayette, he sailed from France and joined Washington's army in 1777. He was made a major general.

In 1780 he was sent south with a force of some 2,000 men to relieve besieged

Charleston, S.C. At the Battle of Camden, S.C., on August 16 he was second in command to Gen. Horatio Gates. When Gates fled the field, Kalb and his men fought off the British force until Kalb fell, with 11 wounds. Three days later he died, a British prisoner. A monument to him was erected in Camden in 1825. His former companion-in-arms, Lafayette, laid the cornerstone.

CHAPTER 27

LAFAYETTE

Among the heroes of the American Revolution only the name of Washington ranks above that of Lafayette. He was a gallant Frenchman who generously placed his life and his fortune at the disposal of the American colonists.

Lafayette was born on Sept. 6, 1757, in Chavaniac, France. His original name was Marie-Joseph-Paul-Yves-Roch-Gilbert du Motier. By birth, he belonged to one of the old noble families of France. His father was killed in battle in 1759. The young man inherited from his father a castle and the title of marquis and from his mother a princely fortune. When he was 16 years old he married into one of the greatest families in France.

Three years later, when Lafayette was 19 and a captain in the French army, came the news that the American colonies had declared their independence of England, France's ancient foe. "At the first news of this quarrel," Lafayette afterward wrote, "my heart was enrolled in it." So he disobeyed the commands of his king and his angry father-in-law,

The Marquis de Lafayette. MPI/Archive Photos/Getty Images

purchased a ship, and after many difficulties sailed for America in 1777. He offered to serve without pay, and Congress gave him the rank of major general. Washington soon became a firm friend—almost a father—to the young Marquis de Lafayette.

Lafayette proved to be a good officer and a wise adviser. He was slightly wounded in his first battle, that of the Brandywine River, in September 1777. The next year he was commended for a masterly retreat from Barren Hill and played an honorable part in the Battle of Monmouth Court House and in the Rhode Island expedition.

More important, however, was his influence in inducing the French government to sign a treaty of alliance with the colonies, in 1778. Without this treaty America could not have won the war. To aid this alliance he was back in France in 1779, but he returned to America in time to assist in the Virginia campaign and in the final movements that led to General Cornwallis' surrender at Yorktown, in 1781.

Lafayette's love for liberty led him to join those French noblemen who favored the Revolution of 1789 in his own country. He was elected to the Estates-General and in that body presented a draft for a Declaration of Rights modeled on the American Declaration of Independence. On the day after the storming of the Bastille on July 14, 1789, he was made commander-in-chief of the new national guard, organized to safeguard the Revolution.

Lafayette rescued Queen Marie Antoinette from the mob that stormed the Palace of Versailles on Oct. 5, 1789, and issued orders to stop King Louis XVI when he sought to escape from France. Gradually Lafayette became dismayed at the growing excesses of the Revolution. As the head of an army raised to defend France against Austria, he planned to overthrow the Jacobins and to support a limited monarchy. The monarchy was overthrown on Aug. 10, 1792, and he was proclaimed a traitor. To escape arrest and the guillotine he fled to Belgium, where he was imprisoned by the Austrians. For five years, from 1792 to 1797, he remained in captivity. Then Napoleon obtained his release.

Lafayette disapproved of the rule of Napoleon and took no part in public affairs until after Napoleon's overthrow. Under the restored Bourbon monarchy, Lafayette generally was politically inactive until the

people were again oppressed. Then he led the opposition, and in 1830 he took part in his third revolution. He commanded the Army of National Guards that drove Charles X from France and placed on the throne Louis Philippe, the "citizen king."

Twice after the close of the American Revolution Lafayette visited the United States—in 1784 and 1824. On the latter visit, Congress voted to give him $200,000 and an additional township of land. This was a welcome gift, for his own property had been taken during the French Revolution.

Lafayette died in Paris on May 20, 1834. His death saddened both the French and the American people. He was neither a great general nor a great statesman. He was, however, a lifelong lover of liberty who played a vital part in three important revolutions.

The Battle of Monmouth during the American Revolution featured the heroic deeds of the woman who became known as Molly Pitcher. In the final years of her life she was honored for her bravery.

Molly Pitcher was born in about 1753. Her original last name is unknown, though she is thought to have been Irish. Military records indicate that her first husband, William Hays, was a gunner in a Pennsylvania artillery regiment in 1777. The nickname "Molly Pitcher" arose during the Battle of Monmouth in New Jersey on June 28, 1778. That day Molly repeatedly carried a pitcher back and forth from a well to cool both the cannons and the exhausted soldiers in her husband's regiment. Legend also has it that Molly took her husband's place at the cannon when he collapsed from the heat.

When Hays died about 1788, Mary (as she was then called) wed John McCauly. Her second husband died about 1813, and thereafter Mary was employed largely as a nurse. On

According to legend, Molly Pitcher took her husband's place at the cannon after he collapsed during the Battle of Monmouth. Library of Congress Prints and Photographs Division

Feb. 21, 1822, Pennsylvania awarded her an annual pension of $40 in recognition of her wartime services. She died on Jan. 22, 1832, in Carlisle, Pa.

Some sources claim that her original name was Mary Ludwig, that she was of German descent, and that her first husband was John Casper Hays. Others claim that Molly Pitcher is purely legendary, a blending of several similar stories of heroic women of the period.

CHAPTER 29

The American naval officer John Barry is one of the men to whom the United States owes its beginnings as a world power on the sea. He won significant maritime victories during the American Revolution and trained many young officers who later became celebrated in the nation's history. He is sometimes called the father of the American Navy.

John Barry was born in County Wexford, Ireland, in about 1745. Little is known of his childhood. It is known, however, that he went to sea as a boy and, in about 1760, made his home in Philadelphia. There he grew wealthy as master and owner of a ship.

Early in the Revolution, in December 1775, Barry received the first captain's commission issued under authority of the Continental Congress and was made commander of the brig *Lexington*. He was the first naval officer to capture a British warship in actual battle, when the British tender *Edward* yielded to the *Lexington* (April 1776). In the winter of 1776–77 he led a troop of volunteers on land in the Trenton and Princeton campaigns.

With a small force of rowboats in 1777 he outmaneuvered the British. He captured some of their transports, cutting off large quantities of supplies from the British Army. In the closing years of the war Barry won more fame as commander of the *Alliance,* a warship of 32 guns. With the *Alliance* in 1781 he captured the British ships *Trepassy* and *Atlanta.*

Barry's outstanding record brought him great prestige, and he was named senior captain when the Navy was reorganized in 1794. This was the highest post in the Navy at that time, and he was popularly called "commodore." Barry was made commander of the flagship *United States* and placed in charge of the West Indies naval forces. He died in Philadelphia on Sept. 13, 1803.

CHAPTER 30

The first great American naval hero was Capt. John Paul Jones. Strong, resourceful, and skilled in seamanship, he loved a battle almost as much as he loved freedom. His words, "I have not yet begun to fight," are famous throughout the world.

John Paul Jones was born on July 6, 1747, near Kirkcudbright, Scotland. His father, John Paul, was a gardener. The boy was christened John Paul, Jr.; he added the "Jones" later. When only 12 years old, he was signed on as an apprentice aboard the *Friendship,* a merchant vessel sailing from England to the American colonies.

When the youth finished his apprenticeship, he joined the British Navy. He did not stay long. At once he saw that no gardener's son, however capable, could rise in the British service. He became first mate on a slaver, a ship that carried slaves, but soon quit. Ashore in the West Indies, he became an actor. In a season he earned enough to sail home as a passenger. On the way, however, the captain and first mate died of typhoid fever. John Paul

Naval hero John Paul Jones is shown posing near a cannon on his ship.
Stock Montage/Archive Photos/Getty Images

was the only man aboard who could navigate. He took the ship into port and the grateful owners kept him on as captain.

At port in the West Indies, Captain Paul had a man flogged for mutinous conduct. The man left the ship, took berth on another, and died some weeks later. Word circulated that he died as a result of the beating. A court of inquiry cleared Paul, but suspicion hung over him. Later, a drunken sailor attacked Paul in his cabin. Drawing his sword only in defense, Paul accidentally ran the man through. The two accidents troubled Paul, and he fled his ship. In Virginia and North Carolina he found old friends. Calling himself Jones, he led the placid life of a planter.

When the Revolution came he rode to Philadelphia and offered his services. He served as first lieutenant on the *Alfred.* His first command was the *Providence;* in 1777 he became captain of the sloop *Ranger.* He carried the news of British Gen. John Burgoyne's surrender at Saratoga to France.

From France he sailed to the west coast of England, destroying coastal shipping and capturing the sloop *Drake.* Back in France, he was given command of the converted merchant ship *Bonhomme Richard.*

Sailing from France he met a convoy off Flamborough Head on England's North Sea coast. The convoy was escorted by the British 44-gun frigate *Serapis*. On the afternoon of Sept. 23, 1779, the *Bonhomme Richard* engaged the *Serapis* in one of the most famous sea battles in history. For hours the ships blazed away at each other at short range. Early in the Battle the *Bonhomme Richard* was badly damaged, and the English captain called upon Jones to surrender. Jones's proud reply has become classic: "I have not yet begun to fight!" Victory came when an American sailor tossed a grenade into a temporary gunpowder magazine located just below the main deck of the *Serapis*.

After the war Jones served the new nation as agent in Europe, and for a brief time he was an admiral in the Russian navy. His health was poor, and he retired to Paris, where he died on July 18, 1792.

CHAPTER 31

"Mad Anthony" Wayne was one of the best generals on the colonial side in the American Revolution. He displayed the most reckless bravery and boldness shown on either side. He calculated his risks carefully, however, and won.

Anthony Wayne was born near Paoli, Pa., on Jan. 1, 1745. He was trained to be a surveyor and served Benjamin Franklin for a short time as an agent in Nova Scotia. When the Revolution began Wayne became a colonel and raised a regiment of volunteers, with whom he served in the disastrous campaign against Quebec. For a time he commanded Fort Ticonderoga, and he was raised to the rank of brigadier general in 1777 for his services there.

His most brilliant exploit of the war was storming the British fort at Stony Point, N.Y., on July 16, 1779. His forces took the strongest British post on the Hudson River with a surprise night attack. This feat won him the thanks of Congress, a gold medal,

Anthony Wayne. **Stock Montage/Archive Photos/Getty Images**

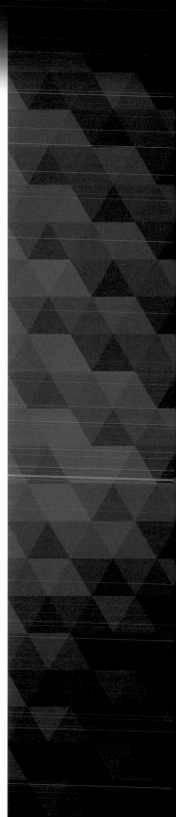

and his nickname, Mad Anthony. In 1790 he was elected to the first of two terms in the Georgia legislature.

Wayne became a major general in 1792 and was sent to fight the Indians of the Ohio Valley. His victory in the Battle of Fallen Timbers on Aug. 20, 1794, led to the treaty of Greenville, which was signed on Aug. 3, 1795. By this treaty the Indians ceded the land that now makes up most of Ohio and parts of Indiana, Michigan, and Illinois. Wayne died at Presque Isle in Lake Erie on Dec. 15, 1796.

CHAPTER 32

CASIMIR PULASKI

The Polish soldier and patriot Casimir Pulaski helped the Americans in their fight for independence. In his own country Pulaski had fought unsuccessfully to keep Poland free from Russian domination.

Pulaski was born to a noble family on March 4, 1747, in Winiary, Poland. He was a hero in the Polish anti-Russian insurrection of 1768, and he distinguished himself defending his country. In 1772 he was falsely accused of plotting to kill the king and was eventually forced to flee to France.

In Paris in late 1776 he met the American statesman Benjamin Franklin, who persuaded him to aid the colonies in their fight for freedom. In mid-1777 Pulaski went to America and joined the colonial army under George Washington. He distinguished himself at the Battle of Brandywine and was commissioned a brigadier general. Pulaski served for some time under Washington and then was given permission to raise an independent corps, the Pulaski Legion. As its leader Pulaski successfully defended Charleston, S.C., from an attack by the British in May 1779. In an attack on Savannah, Ga., on October 9, he received a mortal wound. He died at sea two days later.

Casimir Pulaski. **Archive Photos/Getty Images**

Called "the swamp fox," Francis Marion was one of the boldest and most dashing figures of the American Revolution. Again and again the British were prevented from subduing South Carolina because of the guerrilla warfare waged against them by Marion's men.

Francis Marion was born in South Carolina, probably in St. John's Parish, Berkeley County, in about 1732. When he was about 27, he served in expeditions against the Cherokee Indians. In 1775 he was a member of the South Carolina provincial congress, and when this congress voted to provide money for raising troops he was made a captain. In 1779, by then a lieutenant colonel, he led his regiment in an attack on British positions in Savannah, Ga.

In 1780, taking refuge in forest and swamp, he became the terror of the British in the area around Charleston, S.C. His force, known as Marion's Brigade, ranged from a mere handful to several hundred men. When the enemy was least expecting it, the brigade would dash

Francis Marion's ability to navigate the forests and marshes of South Carolina earned him the nickname "the swamp fox" and allowed him to outmaneuver British forces in the area. MPI/ Archive Photos/Getty Images

out, capture a detachment of British troops or rescue a band of American prisoners, and move swiftly back into hiding. Colonel Banastre Tarleton, the British commander, gave him his nickname when he said that it was impossible to catch the old "swamp fox." In the closing months of the South Carolina campaign, as brigadier general of the militia, Marion cooperated with Gen. Nathanael Greene to win final victory.

In 1781, before the close of the war, Marion was elected to the state senate, and he served several terms in his later years. As a reward for his war service, the state legislature appointed him commander of Fort Johnson at a generous salary. He married a wealthy cousin in 1786. Marion went to the state constitutional convention in 1790. He died on Feb. 26, 1795, in St. John's.

CHAPTER 34

A famous frontiersman and soldier, John Sevier was also a statesman. He was born on Sept. 23, 1745, in Virginia's Shenandoah Valley. After meager schooling he worked as a clerk in his father's fur-trading business. At 16 he married and began his own business. He founded New Market, Va., when he was 19.

Sevier moved his family to the Watauga settlements in Tennessee in 1772. His bravery and leadership in defending the outposts against Indian raids became legendary. In 1780, during the American Revolution, the British forces tried to capture the settlements. On Oct. 7, 1780, Sevier led about 250 frontiersmen in an assault on the British stronghold at King's Mountain, S.C. Sevier's men routed the British.

In 1784 the border settlements were rejected by North Carolina. The Tennessee settlers created a separate state called Franklin, electing Sevier its governor.

Franklin collapsed in 1788. Sevier was imprisoned by North Carolina but later sat in the North Carolina Senate. From 1789 to 1791 he served in Congress. He was governor of Tennessee from 1796 to 1801 and from 1803 to 1809. He served in Congress again from 1811 to 1815. Sevier died while on a surveying commission in Alabama on Sept. 24, 1815.

CHAPTER 35

GEORGE ROGERS CLARK

The vast region now occupied by the states of Ohio, Michigan, Indiana, Illinois, and Wisconsin was won for the United States by the vision and daring of George Rogers Clark. He also won the friendship of the Indians and the French settlers during his expeditions.

Clark was born on a Virginia plantation on Nov. 19, 1752. At the age of 22 he was a surveyor in the Kentucky country, then part of Virginia. He was 25 years old when the American Revolution broke out. In the country west of the Alleghenies, victory depended upon which side the Indians took. The British were stirring up the Indians to attack American settlements. Clark proposed to drive the British from their posts. In the summer of 1778 Clark set out with 175 men and captured three important posts—Kaskaskia and Cahokia on the Mississippi River near St. Louis and Vincennes on the Wabash River.

Clark wintered at Kaskaskia. He learned that a British expedition had retaken Vincennes. On Feb. 7, 1779, he set out on the

George Rogers Clark leads his troops on an attack on Fort Sackville. **Interim Archives/Archive Photos/Getty Images**

180-mile (290-kilometer) journey. On February 23 Clark reached the Wabash with 130 men, though they had run out of food. That night Clark's troops surrounded Fort Sackville, the British post at Vincennes, and opened fire with their long Kentucky rifles. Thinking the American force larger than it was, the British surrendered the next day. The Treaty of Paris in 1783 gave to the United States the land Clark had won. Clark was appointed an Indian commissioner after the war. He died on Feb. 13, 1818, near Louisville, Ky.

CHAPTER 36

The French soldier Rochambeau was one of the officers who aided the American colonists during the American Revolution. He played a major part in the successful siege of Yorktown, Va., that led to the surrender of the British general Charles Cornwallis.

Jean-Baptiste-Donatien de Vimeur, comte de Rochambeau, was born on July 1, 1725, in Vendôme, France. He was educated for the priesthood, but when he was 17 he entered the army. He fought with distinction in several European wars.

After the alliance between France and the American colonies, Rochambeau was made a lieutenant general. In 1780 he was sent with 6,000 men to aid Gen. George Washington. The following year he joined Washington's army on the Hudson River. That summer Cornwallis, harried by the French general Lafayette, took refuge in Yorktown. Rochambeau and Washington joined Lafayette, and Cornwallis surrendered in October 1781.

Rochambeau. **Hulton Archive/Archive Photos/Getty Images**

Rochambeau returned to France in 1783 and was made governor of Picardy and Artois. He took part in the French Revolution and was raised to the rank of field marshal. Disgusted with the excesses of the leaders, he resigned his command. During the Reign of Terror he was imprisoned and narrowly escaped execution on the guillotine. Napoleon restored his estates and rank in 1804. Rochambeau died in Thoré, France, on May 10, 1807.

CHAPTER 37

DEBORAH SAMSON

A remarkable heroine of the American Revolution, Deborah Samson served for more than a year in the Continental Army while disguised as a man. She later lectured on her wartime experiences and was perhaps the first woman to lecture professionally in the United States.

Samson was born on Dec. 17, 1760, in Plympton, Mass. (Her surname, owing to a mistake by an early biographer, has often erroneously been given as Sampson.) Both of her parents were descendants of the *Mayflower* Pilgrims. After spending much of her childhood as an indentured servant, Samson worked as a schoolteacher for a few years.

In 1782 Samson decided to participate in the fight for American independence by joining the Continental Army. Assuming a man's identity, she enlisted in the 4th Massachusetts Regiment in May under the name Robert Shurtleff. Samson quickly earned the respect of her commanding officers and fellow soldiers, who nicknamed her

"Molly" because of her beardless features. She fought in numerous skirmishes and received both sword and musket wounds. A bout with fever eventually uncovered her identity, and she was honorably discharged from the army in October 1783.

In 1784 or 1785 Samson married Benjamin Gannett, a Massachusetts farmer, and was later awarded a small pension by Congress. In 1802 she began making appearances as a lecturer, concluding her highly romanticized speech by dressing in a soldier's uniform and performing the manual of arms. In 1838 Congress passed an act providing full military pension to her heirs. Samson was designated as the official heroine of the Commonwealth of Massachusetts in 1983.

CONCLUSION

The needs of the American colonies in the Revolutionary era brought forward an extraordinary group of leaders. George Washington, as commander-in-chief of the Continental Army, kept the American cause on its feet, inspiring hope by his courage, patience, and firmness during the darkest hours of defeat. To Benjamin Franklin belongs much of the credit for securing aid from France. As an agent of Congress, he used every art of diplomacy to win the goodwill of all classes. Others, such as John Adams and Thomas Jefferson, struggled against discord in Congress and rallied the people against despair. Rarely has a country with so small a population produced so many first-class leaders in a single generation as did the American colonies.

And for every George Washington or Benjamin Franklin, there is a lesser known figure who nevertheless played a vital role in the Revolution. Among them, of course, are numerous soldiers who took part in the fighting itself, but they also include patriots who contributed in various other ways. James Otis and John Dickinson, for example, wrote letters and pamphlets to defend the rights of the colonists and inspire them to the cause. Women such as Lydia Barrington Darragh and Sybil Ludington provided crucial intelligence that helped defend against British attacks. And foremost among the great heroines of the era was Deborah Samson, who disguised herself as a male soldier so she could play her part in the war. In her ideals, her bravery, and her determination, Samson embodied the rousing spirit shared by so many patriots during this remarkable period of American history.

GLOSSARY

acquit To discharge completely (as from an obligation or accusation).

advocate general The senior legal officer.

almanac A publication containing astronomical and meteorological data for a given year and often including a miscellany of other information.

bicameral Having, consisting of, or based on two legislative chambers.

court-martial To subject members of the armed forces or others within its jurisdiction to trial by a court consisting of commissioned officers and in some instances enlisted personnel.

deist One who subscribes to a movement or system of thought advocating natural religion, emphasizing morality, and in the 18th century denying the interference of the Creator with the laws of the universe.

diplomat One employed or skilled in the art and practice of conducting negotiations between nations.

electoral college A body of individuals chosen to elect the president and vice president of the United States.

excise tax Tax levied on the manufacture, sale, or consumption of a commodity.

galvanize To stimulate or excite as if by an electric shock.

garrison A military post.

guillotine A machine for beheading by means of a heavy blade that slides down in vertical guides.

incendiary A person who excites factions, quarrels, or sedition.

Jacobin A member of a radical political group advocating egalitarian democracy and engaging in terrorist activities during the French Revolution of 1789.

levy To impose or collect by legal authority.

martyr A person who sacrifices something of great value and especially life itself for the sake of principle.

militia A body of citizens organized for military service.

privateer An armed private ship licensed to attack enemy shipping.

propagandist One who deliberately spreads ideas, facts, or allegations to further one's cause or to damage an opposing cause.

quartermaster general An officer responsible for the supplies of an army.

ratification Formal approval or sanction.

resolution A formal expression of opinion, will, or intent voted by an official body or assembled group.

surveyor One who studies Earth's surface and measures positions, points, and lines, usually in order to help establish boundaries or make maps.

treason The offense of attempting by overt acts to overthrow the government of the state to which the offender owes allegiance.

writ An order or mandatory process in writing issued in the name of the sovereign or of a court or judicial officer commanding the person to whom it is directed to perform or refrain from performing an act specified therein.

American Historical Association (AHA)
400 A Street SE
Washington, DC 20003-3889
(202) 544-2422
Web site: http://www.historians.org
The AHA serves as a leader and advocate for professionals, researchers, and students in the field of history and upholds academic and professional standards. The AHA also awards a number of fellowships and prizes and offers important resources and publications for anyone interested in the field.

American Independence Museum
One Governors Lane
Exeter, NH 03833
(603) 772-2622
Web site: http://www.independencemuseum.org
The American Independence Museum includes the landmark Ladd-Gilman House and Folsom Tavern, the heart of Exeter's political life during the American Revolution. Exhibits introduce visitors to the social and political life of the time, and collections include early drafts of the Constitution and letters from George Washington.

Canadian Historical Association (CHA)
501-130 Albert Street
Ottawa, ON K1P 5G4
Canada
(613) 233-7885
Web site: http://www.cha-shc.ca
The CHA promotes historical research and
scholarship through its publications, lob-
bying efforts, graduate student support,
and various other endeavors.

National Museum of American History (NMAH)
14th Street and Constitution Avenue, NW
Washington, DC 20002
(202) 633-1000
Web site: http://americanhistory.si.edu
With more than three million artifacts of
American history in its collection, many of
which are on display, the NMAH is dedicated to promoting public interest in the
events that shaped the American nation.

Organization of American Historians (OAH)
112 North Bryan Avenue
Bloomington, IN 47408
(812) 855-7311
Web site: http://www.oah.org

Committed to advancing scholarship in the field of American history, the OAH supports a number of programs, publications, and resources for students, teachers, researchers, and professionals in the field.

WEB SITES

Due to the changing nature of Internet links, Rosen Educational Services has developed an online list of Web sites related to the subject of this book. This site is updated regularly. Please use this link to access the list:

http://www.rosenlinks.com/ioacb/amrevbio

Bobrick, Benson. *Fight for Freedom: The American Revolutionary War* (Atheneum, 2004).

Clark, Charles. *Patriots of the Revolutionary War* (Lucent, 2003).

Fleming, Thomas. *Liberty!: The American Revolution* (Viking, 1997).

Fradin, D.B. *The Signers: The Fifty-six Stories Behind the Declaration of Independence* (Scholastic, 2003).

Furbee, M.R. *Women of the American Revolution* (Lucent, 1999).

Marrin, Albert. *The War for Independence: The Story of the American Revolution* (Atheneum, 1988).

Masters, N.R. *Extraordinary Patriots of the United States of America: Colonial Times to Pre-Civil War* (Roots and Branches, 2010).

Murray, Stuart. *American Revolution*, rev. ed. (DK, 2005).

Rappaport, Doreen, and Verniero, Joan. *Victory or Death!: Stories of the American Revolution* (Scholastic, 2005).

Schmittroth, Linda, and Rosteck, M.K. *American Revolution: Biographies* (UXL, 2000).

INDEX